Alexander Legran's

TRUE SECRETS

of

BLACK MAGIC

PARIS, 1900

2018 translation by Dr. Faustus IV

BLACK MAGIC

THE INFERNAL SPELLS

&

DEMONIC WORKS

Rituals, Grimoires, & Clavicles

Including all of the Secrets of:

Albert the Greater & Lesser

The Red Dragon

&

THE BLACK HEN

Book the Second containing the True

-SANCTUM REGNUM-
of the Key

Or the True Manner
of Making Pacts

With the names, powers, & talents of all of the Great
Spirits, as well as the means of forcing them to appear
through the power of the Great Name. See the chapter
on the great Clavicle which forces entities to obey in whatever
operation you may wish.

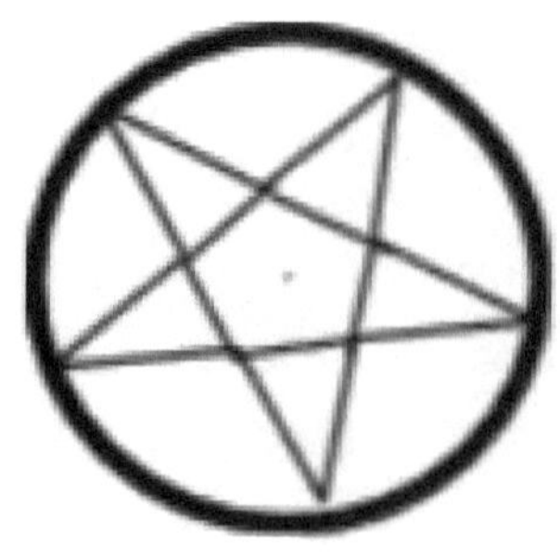

THE SANCTUM REGNUM

Or the True Means of making Pacts with any Spirit whatsoever without it doing you any harm.

The true Sanctum Regnum of the Great Clavicle or Key, also Known as the ***Pacta conventa demonioram*** regarding which so much has been said and written, is an entirely necessary tool for those who wish to compel spirits but who lack the means to create the magic triangle or the Kabbalistic circle. Such persons cannot, I say, arrive at the end of compelling the spirits in the manner to be described hereafter regarding the means of making pacts with any spirit whatsoever, be it to win the favor of the opposite sex, to discover the secrets whispered in any room in the world, to force a demon to do your bidding, to cast storms and hail wherever you please, to render yourself invisible, to be transported anywhere through the very air, to open all locks, to see what transpires in the privacy of any home, to follow the movements of a solitary herdsman, to attain the *Hand of Glory* and to discern the qualities and virtues of all metals and minerals, vegetables, and animals pure and impure, or to do astonishing things, for there is no one who will not be astonished to find that through a pact with the spirits they shall discover all of those secrets of nature which are hidden from most mortals. It is through the use of the *Clavicle of the Great King Solomon* that the true means of making pacts is made clear, and through this alone will ye find the means for acquiring untold riches, for gaining the favors of any man or woman in the world, and for coming to know the impenetrable secrets of Nature through which one can create any sort of good or evil.

We shall commence by revealing the names of the main spirits and their respective powers, and then unfold to our reader the *Pacta demoniorum* whereby the true secret of making pacts with any infernal intelligence whatever is laid bare. Here we show the names and signs of the principle Spirits of the Abyss:

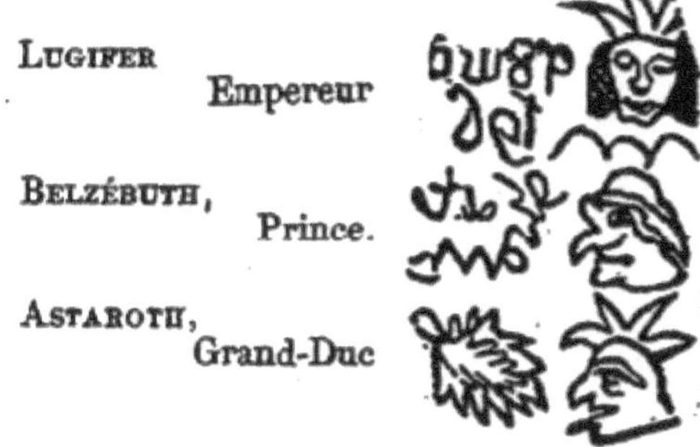

Then come the Superior Spirits who are subordinate to these:

The six spirits named above hold sway over the infernal powers of all

other spirits. In their service we find eighteen subordinate demons:

1. Baël

2. Agares

3. Marbas

4. Pruslas

5. Aamon

6. Barbatos

7. Buer

8. Gusoyn

9. Botis

10. Bathim

11. Pursan

12. Abigar

13. Loray

14. Valefar

15. Forau

16. Ayperos

17. Nuberus

18. Glasyabolas

Having provided the names of these spirits which are inferior to the first six mentioned and described, you will need to know the following:

LUCIFUGÉ commands the first three who are called Baël, Agares and Marbas.

SATANACHIA commands Pruslas, Aamon and Barbatos

AGALLAREPT commands Buer, Gusoyn, and Botis

FLEURETTY commands Bathim, Pursan, and Abigar

SARGATANAS commands Loray, Valofar and Forau

NEBIROS commands Ayperos, Nuberus and Glasyabolas.

And although there be millions of dark intelligences beyond these which are subordinate to the aforementioned, it is useless to name them since they serve the superior spirits as their minions and slaves. Thus while we might seal a pact with the first six spirits we will actually be served by some lesser nameless entity. Nonetheless when making a pact the magician should ask the commanding spirit to put one of his three lieutenants at his or her service.

Here is a precise list of the powers, knowledge, arts and talents of the spirits named above such that when you forge a pact you can do so with the spirit best suited to your needs:

The first is the great ***Lucifuge Rofocale,*** the infernal 'prime minister.' He wields the power given to him by ***Lucifer*** over all riches and treasures of the earth. **Baël** is his minion along with **Agares** and **Marbas**, and there are several thousand lesser demons or spirits in his service.

The second is the great **Satanachia**, a general of the host of Hell. He has the power to make all men and women submit to his will and do as he pleases. He commands a great legion of spirits including **Pruslas**, **Aamon**, and **Barbatos**.

Agalirept is also a general with the power to discover the best hidden secrets wherever they might be whispered. He can unveil the greatest mysteries and he commands a mighty legion of spirits including **Buer, Gusoyn**, and **Botis**.

Fleuretty is best described as a 'lieutenant general' with the power to perform any magical work you please in the space of one night. He also has the power to cast destructive hailstorms. He commands a considerable army of spirits including **Bathim, Pursan** and **Abigar**.

Sargatanas is a sort of 'brigadier' with the power to make one invisible. He can transport you wherever you please and open all locks, and through him you can see what transpires in any home or observe a solitary shepherd among distant hills. He commands **Loray, Valefar** and **Forau**.

Nebiros is a sort of 'aide-de-camp' and 'inspector general' with the power to inflict harm on whoever you may wish. He will help you find the *Hand of Glory* and will teach you the qualities of all metals, minerals, and plants, as well as all animals pure and impure. It his he who teaches the art of seeing the future as he is the greatest Necromancer among the infernal spirits. He goes everywhere and inspects all infernal projects, and he commands **Ayperos, Nuberus**, and **Glasyabolas** among others.

-The Great Summons-

For calling upon those Spirits with which you would make a pact as it is found in the Great Clavicle.

Being in your laboratory or some secret place removed from mankind (an old ruin for example, since the spirits have the power to bring you any treasure you please) you shall trace a **magic triangle** with your bloodstone, but only for your initial pact. Then place two blessed candles beyond those candles which will be placed around the triangle in a manner soon to be described. Place a crucifix just beyond these so that the spirits cannot harm you. Now toss your request into the middle of the triangle while holding your magic wand in the other hand. The paper should contain the **Great Summons to the Spirit**, the demand you make of him, the text of the pact, and the text for the dismissal of the Spirit.

-The Great Summons-

"**Emperor Lucifer,** master of all rebel spirits, I pray you to show me favor in summoning your prime minister **Lucifugé Rofocale** as I desire to make a pact with him. I also pray you, **Prince Belzebuth**, to protect me in my enterprise. **Count Astorth** show me favor and make it such that on this night the great Lucifugé shall appear in a human form and without foul odor, and that he shall accord me by means of the pact the wealth of which I stand in need. Oh great **Lucifugé**, I pray you to quit your abode wherever it be to come and speak with me, or I shall be forced to compel you by the power of the great and living God and his Son and the Holy Ghost. Obey forthwith or you will be tormented through the power of the mighty words of the **Clavicle of Solomon** which compels all rebel spirits to obey. Appear as soon as possible or I shall pursue you without cease, and you shall be tormented by the mighty words of the Clavicle:

"Agion, Telagram, vaycheon stimulamaion y ezpares retragrammaton oryoram irion esytion existion eryona onera brasim moyn messias soter Emanuel Saboot Adonay, te adoro et invoco."

Once you have recited the words of power indicated above, the spirit will appear to you.

The Spirit Appears

"Here We stand, what then dost thou desire? Why dost thou disturb Our repose? Speak!"

This is LUCIFUGÉ ROFOCALE

Say to the Spirit:

"I ask to seal a pact with you such that you can make me wealthy, and if not I shall torment you with the mighty words of the Clavicle."

The Spirit responds:

"We cannot give thee what thou asketh unless thou dost yield unto Us twenty years during which time We shall do as We please with thine body and soul."

Now you shall throw your pact to him. It is to be written with your own hand using your own blood as ink on a piece of virgin parchment. It will consist of the words which follow and your signature.

This is the PACT:

"I swear to recompense the great **Lucifuge** in twenty years time for all of the treasures he shall render unto me. In good faith I sign my name."

-Your Signature

Lucifuge:

"We cannot give to thee that which it is thou ask of Us."

To force the spirit to obey you, you must rely upon the **Great Summons** using the mighty words of the **Clavicle,** intoning them until the spirit reappears, at which point he will say something like the following:

2nd Appearance of the Spirit:

"Why dost thou continue to torment Us? If you leave Us in peace We shall grant unto thee the nearest available treasure, provided that thou dost sacrifice one coin of it on the first Monday of each month to Us, and that thou doth call upon Us but one day per week between the hours of midnight and two. Take up your pact, for behold We have signed it, and if thou dost not honor it thou shalt be wholly Ours in the space of twenty years."

Say to the Spirit:

"*I acquiesce to your demand provided you show me the nearest treasure such that I can take it immediately.*"

Response of the Spirit:

"*Follow then, and take such treasure as We will show to you.*"

Then you shall follow the spirit along the route indicated into magic triangle, and you will not be afraid. Throw your pact signed and sealed upon the treasure trove and touch it with your magic wand. Take as much as you can hold and return via the triangle. Set your treasure down and immediately begin to read the spell for the dismissal of the Spirit as it is written here.

Spell for dismissing the Spirit with whom you have a pact:

"*Oh Great **Lucifugé**, I am content with you for now, and I leave you in peace and allow you to retire as you see fit without making a sound or leaving behind a fetid odor. Think well upon the terms of our pact, for if you break it for an instant you will be tormented eternally by the great and powerful words of the **Clavicle of King Solomon** which compels all rebel spirits to obey.*"

Prayer to the Almighty to work through the action of the Graces:

"All powerful God, celestial father who has created all things for their service and utility to man, I thank you very humbly for the actions of the Graces through whom you have in your great goodness permitted me to make a pact with the rebel spirits without risk and so compel them to give me that which I require. I thank you all powerful God for the blessing you have granted me this night. See fit to accord me, wretched creature that I am, your precious favors. It is now, oh Lord, that I come to know the true power of your great promises when you said unto humanity: 'Seek, and ye shall find, knock and it shall be opened unto you.' As you have commanded and beseeched us to show charity to the poor, see fit to inspire me to acts of generosity and make it such that I will pour a part of the resources you have seen fit to grant me into holy works you see fit for me to fulfill. Make it such that I enjoy these riches in peace, and let not some rebel spirit mislead me into losing myself in the gold of which you have seen fit to make me the master. Inspire in me, Oh Lord, the sense needed to avoid the snares of the Evil One and all of his minions. I place myself, oh Lord and Father, Son, and Holy Ghost under your holy protection. Amen."

-Oraison for protection against Evil Spirits-

"Oh Father Almighty! Oh Mother most tender! Oh you example of tenderness to all Mothers! Oh Son who art the flower of all Sons! Oh form of *forms! Soul, spirit, harmony and name of all things, conserve and protect us and be propitious to us in all things! Amen."*

-THE CONJURING OF THE FOUR-

"Caput mortuum, imperet tibi Dominus per vivum et devotum Serpentum-- Cherub imperet tibi Dominus per Adam Iothavah!-- Aquila errons, imperet tibi Dominus per alas Tauri!-- Serpens imporet tibi Dominus.-- Tetragrammaton per Angleum et Leonum!

Michael, Gabriel, Raphael, Anaël.

Fluat udor par spiritum Eloïm.

Maneat Terra per Adam Iotchavah.

Fiat Firmamentum per Iahnvehu-Zeboath.

Fiat Judicium per ignem in virtute Michael.

Oh dark Angel of the dead eyes, obey or be soaked in this holy water.

Winged Bull, work and return to the earth if you do not wish to be skewered by this sword.

Wild Eagle, obey this sign or be born away by the wind.

Roving Serpent, coil at my feet or be tormented by the Sacred Fire and evaporate with the smoke of the incense I now burn.

Let water return to water, let fire burn, let the air swirl about, and let the earth fall upon the earth by virtue of the Pentagram which is the Morning Star, and in the name of **Tetragrammaton** which is writ in the center of the luminous cross, Amen."

-THE CONJURING OF THE SEVEN-

"In the name of Saint Michael, thou art commanded by Jehovah to be gone from here Chavajoth!

In the name of Saint Gabriel, thou art commanded by Adonaï to be gone from here Belial!

In the name of Holy Raphael, thou art commanded by Elchim to be gone from here, Sachabiel!

By Samuel Zebaoth and in the name of Eloïm Gibor, begone from here Adrameleck!

By Zachariel and Sachiel-Melech, obey the will of Elva, Samgabiel!

By the divine and human name of Schaddai and the sign of the Pentagram that I hold in my right hand, in the name of the angel Anael, through the power of Adam and Heves who are Iotchavah, withdraw oh Silith, ind leave us in peace! Nahema! By the holy Eloïm and the genius of Cashiel, Schaltiel, Aphiel, Zarahiel, and by the command of Orifiel, turn away from us, oh moloch! We shall offer up no children for you to devour!

OCCULT PRACTICES & MARVELOUS SECRETS

We have gathered from the mighty grimoires a certain number of spells of a highly curious nature, the efficacy of which has been attested to by many of the wise ancients. We provide them below in no particular order. Our magical supply shop is at the service of our readers when it comes time to purchase the various essential ingredients which we have carefully prepared while scrupulously following all of the prescribed rituals.

-LIST OF SPELLS-

Agatha. The agatha, which is consecrated to **Mercury**, removes all perils and moves one to generosity.

Eagle. Those eat the brain of the eagle crushed in the juice of hemlock will fight on without hope of truce. The eagle is consecrated to *Jupiter.*

Lover's stone. A man may come to know whether a woman has been true through this. He places the lover's stone beneath her pillow and if she be true she will caress him. If she be false she will jump to the bottom of the bed.

If you wish to force the inhabitants from a house, take powder from this stone and rub it on four lumps of coal which you must then place at the four corners of the domicile. All of the inhabitants will depart in haste, even those who had been asleep. The lover's stone is consecrated to **Saturn.**

Alum. If you rub some cloth with the white of an egg mixed with some alum after having washed it with some salty water, then allow it to dry, it will keep all fire from burning.

If you take some *red arsenic* and alum and boil them together and mix them with the juice of rhubarb and the gum that oozes from the laurel tree, you can shake a man's hand and be able to manipulate him, or take a hot iron in your hand without being burned.

Amethyst. The amethyst keeps one from becoming drunk and opens up the secrets of science, and it is consecrated to *Mars.*

Eels. If you place several eels in a pot of wine and allow them to die, whoever drinks of this wine shall hate wine for a year and may never drink again in his life.

Future. Take the dried blood of an ass and mix it with the fat from the teats of a lynx in equal parts, making little pellets with which you shall perfume your house. When this is done someone will appear to you in sleep and tell you the things to come.

Beryl. When you wear it on your person you can win any trial, and it helps children advance in their studies. It is consecrated to *Jupiter.*

Goat. If you plunge some glass into a boiling mix of vinegar and goat's blood the glass will become like butter. If you sprinkle yourself with this mixture you will have frightful hallucinations. If you throw it on the fire in the presence of a person with epilepsy, he will have a fatal convulsion if you then show him the lover's stone. The same man would be healed by just a few drops of eagle's blood in some water. The goat is consecrated to *Venus.*

Chalcedony. Worn about the neck it banishes all illusions. It is consecrated to **Saturn.**

Hair. To make your hair grow burn some bees and mix their ashes with some mouse droppings, then infuse this mixture into some rosato oil. Add walnut ashes or burnt beans and hair will grow wherever you apply the mixture.

Chrysolite. When mounted in gold it prevents fear, protects against phantoms and moves one to wise conduct without excesses and sensual ardor. When placed under the tongue during a fever it removes thirst. It is consecrated to the **Sun.**

Rooster. To keep him from crowing anoint his crest and head with oil. To keep him from coupling anoint his vent with oil.

Coral. This will keep you safe when on the water (against shipwreck, storms, and all accidents). It bestows good judgement and prudence. It is consecrated to the **Moon.**

Rock crystal (quartz). When placed out in the sun it can set combustibles ablaze. A nurse can dip it in honey and eat the honey or even swallow bits of the stone and she will see her milk increase. It is consecrated to the **Moon.**

Devil. To make a sleeping person see the devil, sprinkle the blood of the hoopoe bird upon his face. He will think himself surrounded by devils!

Diamond. The diamond grants victory over enemies and causes dangerous beasts to flee. Conflicts will end to your advantage and practical jokes or schemes against you will founder, above all when you wear it on your left side. It is consecrated to **Mars.**

Enchant animals. If you wish to make an animal do your bidding you should go to its stall and tickle its forehead with that flower known as the *squill.* If you melt some wax onto the horns of a calf the animal will follow you wherever you wish without trouble (Aristotle).

Hellebore. The juice heals leg ailments, kidney trouble, and bladder defects. The root exorcises haunted houses. If you cook the root and keep it in a white linen cloth it cures dark thoughts and obsessions.

Emerald. The stone imparts knowledge, memory, and the ability to see the future. It can help you to acquire a fortune. When placed under the tongue it bestows the gift of prophecy, as it inspires intuition and true seeing. It is consecrated to **Mercury.**

*The **Red Water lily**.* This is consecrated to the sun, and it brings light to the darkness.

*The **euphorbus**.* This plant cures ailments of the head and stomach. It heals ulcers of the skin, hemorrhoids, and diarrhea. It is consecrated to **Mars**.

Woman. It is written in the *Book of Cleopatra* that a woman who is not content with her spouse can, if she wishes, take the pad from the left foot of a wolf and wear it about on her person. In this way she is certain to be satisfied and the man will adore her exclusively.

To make a woman admit to something, place a frog in some eau-de-vie and then pluck out its tongue before returning the tongue to the liquor. Apply the tongue to the region of the heart when the woman is asleep and she will respond to all questions.

Frog. A frog's tongue placed under the pillow will cause a person to talk in their sleep. The frog is consecrated to the **Moon**.

Mistletoe. Joined with slypium it can open locks. Hung from a tree with the wing of a swallow it will cause all sorts of birds to gather.

Marshmallow. The seed of the marshmallow can be mashed and formed into a lotion which can be applied to the face and hands to ward off stings from wasps and bees.

Heliotrope herb. It is consecrated to the sun and must be gathered in July and August when the sun is in the sign of *Leo.* It is worn about on one's person enclosed in a wolf's tooth and wrapped up in a laurel leaf. If you carry it inside of a church you cannot be slandered, and women in the church who have been unfaithful to their husbands will be unable to leave. If placed under your pillow the talisman will show you in dreams those persons who have a secret to tell you.

Heliotrope stone. (Also the precious *Stone of Babylon* which was used to interpret oracles). If you anoint yourself with water from the flower of the same name you will see the sun shine through the stone blood red. It is consecrated to the *Sun.*

Magical Herbs. Only gather these herbs from the 23rd to the 29th of June. Name the use you have for each herb as you pluck it. Keep your herbs under some wheat or barley until you are ready to use them. The main magical herbs are as follows:

Heliotrope, henbane, nepte, nettles, small teasel, celandine, periwinkle, houndstongue, lily, mistletoe, centaurea, verbena, melissa, serpentine.

Owl. If you place an owl's heart on the left side of a woman's chest while she sleeps she will reveal all of her secrets. The owl is consecrated to the **Moon**.

Hoopoe. If you carry the head of the hoopoe bird about in a little sack, those with whom you do business can never deceive you. If you carry only the eyeballs of the bird you will grow fatter, and if you wear the eyeballs in a pouch over your stomach you will make peace with all of your enemies. The Hoopoe is consecrated to **Saturn**.

Hyacinthe. This will keep you safe from lightning and plague.

Jasper. Jasper stops hemorrhages.

Henbane. Henbane heals ulcers, and when worn as a talisman it prevents them. When crushed it calms the gout and above all if one is born under a sign of the zodiac with feet or hooves. When mixed with some sugar the juice heals liver ailments (since the plant is consecrated to *Jupiter*) and it will break any silver vessel it is poured into. When mixed with the blood of a rabbit in a rabbit-skin flask it will cause many rabbits to gather in one place.

Lamp. If you wish for a palace and all within it to appear as black you must take a lamp's wick and soak it in a rough and foamy sea before drying it well and then using it.

If you wish to make it seem as if none of the occupants of a room have a head, pour some yellow sulfur into a lamp where you have also mixed some sulfur with the oil. Light the lamp and place it in the midst of all assembled.

If you make a taper from a funeral shroud and light it in the middle of a room you will see marvelous things indeed.

Catch a green frog and lop off its head over a funeral shroud, then soak the whole in elderberry oil. Use this as a wick to burn in a green lamp and you shall behold the form of a black man holding forth a lamp along with a number of other startling things.

If you wish to make a room appear as if it were full of serpents, acquire some snake fat and mix it with salt, then take a swath of funeral shroud that you have cut into quarters and apply the fat to each rag. Make these strips into wicks for four lamps which you must then burn in each corner of a room with some elderberry oil in a new lamp, and the desired effect will be achieved.

Dog's tongue. If you combine a dog's tongue and a frog's womb together in a place, dogs will gather in that place. If you wear a big toe as a talisman dogs will never bark at you. If you hang this same talisman around a dog's neck he shall chase his tail until he dies of exhaustion.

Lapis lazuli. Worn about on your person it heals hypochondria and fever. It is consecrated to Venus.

Lion. To make all of your enemies flee from you, be they man or beast, you must wear a belt made from a lion's skin or carry the eyeballs of a lion under your armpit. The urine of a lion when taken for three consecutive days will cure a fever. The lion is consecrated to the **Sun.**

White Lily. The white lily heals kidney, eye, and stomach ailments. The juice aids digestion and heals shingles. The lily helps the eyes because it is consecrated to *Venus*. It must be gathered in July.

Wolf. To keep wolves from entering a village, bury a wolf's tail at the approach to town and at the doors to the stables to keep your animals safe. The wolf is consecrated to *Mars*.

Melissa. If you wear it about on your person you gain charisma. Hang it around a bull's neck and he will become obedient.

Night. If you anoint your face with the blood of a bat you will be able to see and read at night as you would during the day.

Birds. If you wish to take a bird in hand take any kind of grain and soak in the lees of wine and some hemlock juice. Cast this seed upon the ground and the birds who eat it will not be able to fly away.

If you wish to hear the song of invisible birds take two caged birds into the woods along with some dogs and act as if you are on the hunt. Do this on the 5th of November. Catch the first animal you come upon and bring it home, then eat it along with the heart of a fox. You will immediately hear the singing of birds, and if you wish to have others present hear the singing you merely have to kiss them.

Nettle. Hold it in your hand with some yarrow and you will not fear ghosts. (Gather these from the 10th of July to the 23rd of August). Mix nettle juice with some serpentine and sprinkle it on your hands, then cast the rest upon the ground. You can then kneel down and take up the fish you will find there.

Periwinkle. Crush this with some earthworms then slip it into the food of the one whose love you wish to win.

THE BLACK HEN

Take a ***black hen*** that has never laid eggs and that a rooster has never mounted. Make certain that when you seize her she makes no sound, and toward this end go to the coop late at night when she is asleep. Grab her by the neck so that she cannot make a noise and squeeze as hard as you must. Find a crossroads and, at the stroke of midnight, make a circle with your magic wand made of cypress wood. Place the hen's body in the circle and chop it in half while pronouncing these words three times: *"Eloïm, Essaïm, frugativi et appellavi."*

Turn to face the east, then kneel and say a prayer. Now speak the *GREAT SUMMONS* and an otherworldly spirit will appear before you in a scarlet garment bedecked with braid, a yellow vest and sea-green leggings. His head will be like that of a dog with the ears of an ass, and he shall have horns. His legs will be those of a cow. He will ask what your demand might be and you shall tell him what you see fit. He cannot refuse your demands and he can make you the richest and happiest of mortals.

Fleas. To rid a room of fleas, sprinkle it with a mixture of rue and mare's urine (Pliny).

Bedbugs. To be rid of bedbugs take a cucumber shaped like a snake, pickle it, rinse it, and use it to sprinkle your bed with water. You can also use a bull's pizzle soaked in vinegar. To capture bedbugs alive without touching them place a leaf of comfrey by your bedside and they will gather beneath it and go nowhere else.

Quintefeuille. When worn on your person it will make you succeed in all things. Its juice eases tooth and stomach aches. Its root heals sores and abrasions when applied as a plaster, and when the juice is mixed with water it can cure the scrofula. It is consecrated to **Mercury**.

Rats. You can rid your house of rats by burning the hoof of a horse or mule therein.

Knotweed. Knotweed cures heart and stomach ailments while it enlivens the respiration and circulation. This root is sexual tonic and it heals eye problems. The juice can be used to attract love. It is consecrated to the **Sun**.

Erotic Dreams. To be rid of these make the sign of the cross on your stomach with a blade made of lead.

Sapphire. Sapphire brings inner peace and peace with others. It lends devotion and quenches passion. It regenerates a man and heals anthrax and snakebite. The sapphire is consecrated to **Jupiter**.

Sterility. To ensure that a woman remains barren take a child's baby teeth and encase them in silver before convincing her to wear them around her neck. Every month you should drink a glass of mule's urine. Wear the finger of a stillborn fetus around your neck.

Red spots. A cow's bile mixed with egg shells and dissolved in vinegar (to apply to the skin).

Mole. Take a mole's foot and enfold it in a laurel leaf. If placed in a nest this keeps eggs from developing. If placed in a horse's mouth the beast will flee. To catch a mole put an onion in his hole along with a pear and some garlic. After a short time he will come out willingly. To chase moles from a field, sprinkle one mole with some sulfur and set fire to it. To make a black horse turn white wash him with some water in which you have boiled a mole. The mole is consecrated to ***Saturn.***

The turtledove. If you wear the heart of a turtledove around on your person sewn up in some wolf's skin it serves as an anti-aphrodisiac. The ashes from the heart of a turtledove sprinkled on eggs will keep them from hatching. If you take some water in which a mole was boiled, add the blood of a turtledove and wash a dappled horse with it you will see all of the black hairs fall out. A tree where a turtledove perches will no longer bear fruit. The turtledove is consecrated to ***Venus.***

Turquoise. Turquoise protects you from falling off of a horse.

Sea calf. A mixture of water, sea-calf blood and bits of sea-calf heart will draw fish to the spot. If placed under a dish it gives one marvelous judgement, and a criminal who does this is sure to be treated with indulgence. The sea-calf is consecrated to **Venus.**

Verbena. When made into a plaster verbena cures scrofula, incontinence of the bladder, sores and hemorrhoids. When worn about to the exclusion of all other herbs it increases sexual vigor. When consumed as a tea it facilitates digestion and pufies the breath.

Placed in a home, a field, or a vineyard it augments productivity and revenue.

It is consecrated to Venus and must be gathered in March when the **Sun** is in the sign of the **Ram.**

SECRETS OF THE

MAGICAL ARTS

of Albert the Greater & the Lesser

-THE GRIMOIRE-

The Composition of Death

-or-

THE PHILOSOPHER'S STONE

Take a new terracotta pot and place a pound of copper within it. Add a pint of acid and bring it to a boil for half an hour. Now add three ounces of vert-de-gris and boil for an hour. Add two and one half ounces of arsenic and boil for another hour. Add three ounces of well-pulverized oak bark and allow the mix to boil for another thirty full minutes, then add some rosewater and boil for twelve minutes. Add three ounces of soot and allow to boil until the composition is good, and to see if it is ready you should dip a nail in the liquid. If the color of the nail changes you should remove it and the liquid will produce a pound and a half of good gold. If the nail is untouched the formula is not yet ready.

-MAGIC MIRROR-

This mirror is made of two panes of glass. It is flat on one side and convex on the other. The two sides are called the small and large sides respectively. The mirror is used in various counter-magic operations in order to make known your attacker. You must look at yourself on one side and then on the other while pronouncing the words indicated, and at the right moment your own image will disappear and will be replaced by the image of your magical adversary. His image will come and go several times.

The magic mirror also possesses certain natural virtues such as being able to heal extreme pain and rheumatism in general. To gain this effect the part of the body where the pain resides must touch the mirror directly first on one side and then on the other without regard to which side of the mirror you begin with. Each time the patient touches the mirror you should call upon three saints, for example "*St. Joseph, St. John, St. James*, I beseech you to heal this person (give the name of the afflicted.)" Repeat this three times and then say **Pater** three times, then **Ave** three times before making the sign of the cross. Instruct the patient to wipe the affected area once daily with fingers moistened with saliva for three consecutive days, and have him say *Pater* and *Ave* as indicated above.

This mirror should not be used for any profane purposes.

To Destroy an Enemy or to discover
a hidden adversary with the Magic Mirror

Buy a new terracotta pot with a cover along with some camphor and some needles, then obtain the heart of a calf or a cow. All of this should be done without haggling.

Bar the door to your laboratory.

Place the heart on a clean plate and jab all of your needles into it repeating the following as each needle is inserted:

"*Against whomsoever it may be (if you know you should say the name instead) one time vassis atatlos vesul et cremus, verbo sans bergo bibolia herbonos, twice vassis atatlos, etc., thrice vassis, etc.*"

With this done place the heart in a cooking pot at exactly 11:30 pm and let it boil until one hour after midnight at the least. The next day you must bury the pot in the earth in an uncultivated spot.

To see your hidden adversary allow the pot to boil until all of the water is gone as you repeat the words indicated above every five minutes while looking into the mirror, now from one angle and now from another. It is rare not to see your adversary pass rather often.

Note: You must not leave your house during this operation and care must be taken that no one else leaves. You must perform a *novena,* which is to say that for the nine following days running you must repeat the words indicated above at half-past the hour of Eleven.

TO REMOVE ALL SPELLS & TO CAUSE THE MALEFACTOR TO SHOW HIMSELF TO YOU.

Take the heart of an already dead animal being sure not to harm it in any way and place it on on clean plate. Take nine toothpicks of hawthorn wood and proceed as follows:

Stick one pick in the heart saying: "*Adibaga, Sabaoth, Adonay, contra ratout prisons pererunt fini unixio paracle gossum.*"

Now insert two more picks saying: "*Qui fussum mediator agras gaviol valax.*"

Now insert two more saying: "*Landa azazar valoi sator xio paracle gossum.*"

Now insert two more saying: "*Avir sunt (before you) paracletur stator verbonum offisum fiando.*"

Now continue: "*I call upon those who created the Missel Abel, from everywhere come and find us by land and by sea, from every corner of the world, without delay or hesitation.*"

With these last words pierce the heart with a nail. Note that if you cannot find hawthorn toothpicks you can use new nails instead. When the heart has been pierced in the manner indicated you should place it in a little sack and hang it over some thoroughfare but very high in the air so that it will not be seen. The next day take the heart down and put it on a plate. Take out the first toothpick and stick it back in at another location pronouncing the same words indicated earlier, and continue on in this way until the process has been completed without ever using the same hole twice. Continue on with this same operation for nine days.

When this is done and the last nail is in the heart you must make a great fire, roasting the heart on a metal grill. The evildoer will come to you asking for mercy. If he does not come to you within a short time he will die. Note well that you must avoid barring the door or keeping the malefactor away by any means.

TO BREAK & DESTROY ALL <u>*COMMON SPELLS AGAINST ANIMALS.*</u>

Take a cup of salt, more or less, according to the number of animals affected and pronounce the following words:

"Hergo gomet hune gueridans sesserant deliberant amci."

Now make three passes around the animals starting from the east. Face the animals all the while and sprinkle the salt upon them pinch by pinch as you recite the words above.

A TALISMAN: <u>*ITS PREPARATION & VIRTUES*</u>

On the *Eve of St. John* between the hours of one and two in the morning go forth to where some periwinkle grows. It can be in your garden or in a flower pot, but the important thing is that it be out under the open sky. Gather the plant without saying a word and bring it into your house. Take care not to look behind you, even if you hear the sound of footsteps right at your heels. Besides no harm may come to one during this operation and even wild animals will flee from the magician thus employed. Preserve the periwinkle in order to use it in the following operation:

When you take your bunch of periwinkle out of its receptacle, snatch up the first branch you lay eyes upon. Remove the head of the flower and place it on some white paper, then pull off some leaves and the stem until you have nine pieces of the plant. Add camphor such that the whole packet will weigh about a pound and fold it up. When you have folded it such that the contents cannot be seen, begin to intone these words as you fold the paper further:

If you wish to use the packet as a talisman say "*For X (name a person) residing at Y, who we wish to see safe against all curses, for X one time vassis atatlos vesul et cremus, verbos san hergo dibolia herbonos, twice vassis atatlos, etc, thrice vassis, etc.*" Repeat three times.

If you wish to use it to break or destroy a spell say " *For X residing at Y from whom we wish to remove any curse or spell whatsoever, once vassis atatlos vesul et cremus, verbo san hergo dibolia herbonos twice vassis, thrice vassis, etc.*" Repeat three times.

The paper should be resting on the flat side of your magic mirror as you make your packet, and once it is finished you should place it on the convex side before giving it to the person in question.

If the packet is to serve as a talisman the beneficiary should take it in her right hand and make the sign of the cross, then keep it tucked away in her clothes at all times. It will work for one year, after which it should be thrown on the fire. If the packet is meant to break a spell the beneficiary should again take it in her right hand, make the sign of the cross, and place it on her person where there is some infirmity. Keep it there for three to five days. At the end of this time the affected person or the magician can take the packet, make the sign of the cross, and throw it into the fire. Cover it with coals and leave immediately. As you set foot outside say: "*May God Keep Us.*"

TALISMANS & AMULETS

For joy, beauty, and strength of body: Have an amulet with an image of **Venus** graven upon it, which is a woman holding apples and flowers in her hand. On the other side you can have an image of the scales, *Pisces* the fish, or *Taurus* the bull.

To heal the gout: Have an amulet made with an image of the *Pisces* upon it, one head up and the other down. It shall be of gold or silver or a mixture of the two, and it should be made when the sun is in *Pisces.*

To have a subtler mind and a better memory: For this obtain an amulet with the image of *Mercury* graven upon it along with the image of *Gemini* or *Virgo* on the other side.

In his treatise on precious stones **KING SOLOMON** tells us that the image of a warrior treading upon snakes will make a man invincible if it be graven upon green jasper and set in brass, then worn about the neck.

When etched in stone and set in an iron ring the image of *Scorpio* and *Sagittarius* fighting will cause division among those touched by the wearer.

The figure of the *Ram* with half of *Taurus* when graven upon a stone and set in silver brings peace and concord.

The figure of the *Water-Bearer* engraved in turquoise brings merchants all that they want.

The presence of a figure of **Mars** etched into a precious stone makes men lust for war.

The figure of **Jupiter** makes men amiable, gracious, and open to receiving that which he desires.

The figure of **Capricorn** etched into a stone and set in a silver ring makes a man invulnerable in his person and property

The best day for making **talismans of luck** is the Wednesday nearest August 21.

The **talismans of love** should be made on April 26th, August 15th, and the 12th of September.

On this last date one can create a very effective talisman: Choose the hour of Venus and the day of Venus nearest the 12th and inscribe the characters of Venus on a plaque of red copper having prepared it under her influence. Make of this a medallion which you should take care to put around your neck each day before sunrise suspended from a cord twisted from some portion of the desired lady's underclothes. Stand before her door and pronounce the following word twelve times: **Amapoyflac.** Do this each morning for the entire month of October and on the 1st of November she will come to give herself to you.

Talismans of war are made in October during the days and hours of Mars, and the 22nd of October is a very propitious day for their fabrication.

A talisman in the shape of a pentacle brings good fortune to those who work in the fields, especially when made during a new moon in December on the day and at the hour of *Saturn.*

A talisman bearing the mark of *Jupiter* and made from steel is made in February on the day and during the hour of *Mars.*

BREAKING ATTACK SPELLS WITH THE THE BLACK ROOSTER

Take a black rooster and force three drops of holy water into his beak, then kill him and hang him by his legs in a barn for three full days. When the days have passed take him by the legs and bury him in warm dung such that no one may find him and extract him. Whoever is using magic against you will fall ill and die slowly over the course of 6 months to one year.

When performing the above spell pronounce the following words of power: "Against such and such a person, once vassis, etc.

TO SPELLBIND YOUR ENEMY
& CAUSE HIM TO SUFFER

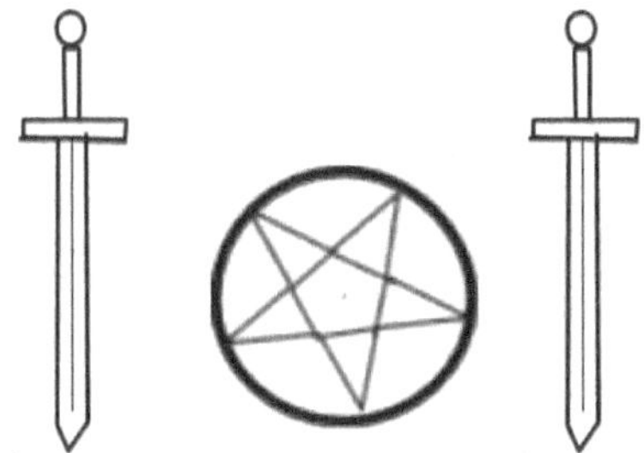

Go to a cemetery and find an old coffin nail. Take it in your left hand and say: *"Nail I take you in order that you may serve me and undo and harm whoever I wish, in the name of the Father, the Son, and the Holy Ghost, Amen."*

When you wish to make use of it, trace the figure shown below on a piece of virgin parchment with some red charcoal and cast the nail into the center of the triangle as you recite the following:

"L'ater noster jusqu'a in terra."

Now tap the nail with a rock while saying: *"Do harm unto X person until I take you from this spot."* Cover the place with some dust and remember where it is, since you can undo any harm inflicted by removing the nail and saying:

"I remove you such that the harm to X person will cease in the Name of the Father, the Son, and the Holy Ghost, Amen." Take up the nail and efface the image, not with the hand that cast the spell but with the other, otherwise there will be some danger posed to the spellcaster.

Work this spell on the last Friday of the month early in the morning.

Spell to cause suffering.

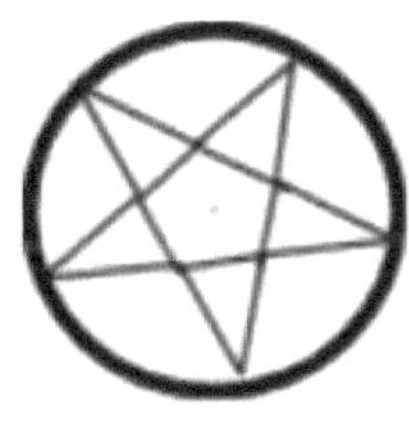

Take a portion of lard the size of an egg and stab it with pins (about 30 give or take) while reciting words such as: "Once vassis statios etc." Bless two twigs and form them into a cross, then carry this all far beyond cultivated land.

Protection for horses

Pass your hand across a horse's stomach and say: "Oh horse should you have sores or colic or the 36 other afflictions of your race, may God heal you with the help of blessed Saint Eloy. In the name of the Father, the Son, and the Holy Ghost, Amen." Now say five *Our Fathers* and five *Hail Marys* on your knees before having your horse swallow a handful of grey salt dissolved in a liter of tepid Holy Water.

To heal a tumor or any other affliction
<u>That can be seen or touched.</u>

With your longest finger circle the afflicted spot thrice, saying with each pass: "Evil affliction, it is said that you have as many roots here as God has helpers in Heaven." Do this three days in a row before the sun rises. As you make a circle with your finger be sure that it does not leave the skin.

Against Burns

"Saint Lazarus and Our Lord Jesus Christ went into a holy city. Saint Lazarus said to the Lord: 'On high I hear a great noise.' Our Lord said unto him: 'It is a child burning, go to him and heal him of his suffering.'" Repeat this passage thrice over burnt skin and each time blow on the affected area, then apply a compress soaked through with olive oil.

To Return Stolen Objects

Burn a goodly handful of rue and speak the words "Believe in God" three times while making the sign of the cross to the front and back.

To see at night a vision of what shall come To pass or what has come to pass.

When night comes trace the figure below on some virgin parchment. The two Ns indicate the place where you must write your name, as well as what you wish to know.

The free space between the two circles is set aside for the names of the Angels you want to invoke. When this is done recite the oraison below and sleep on your right side with the parchment under your pillow.

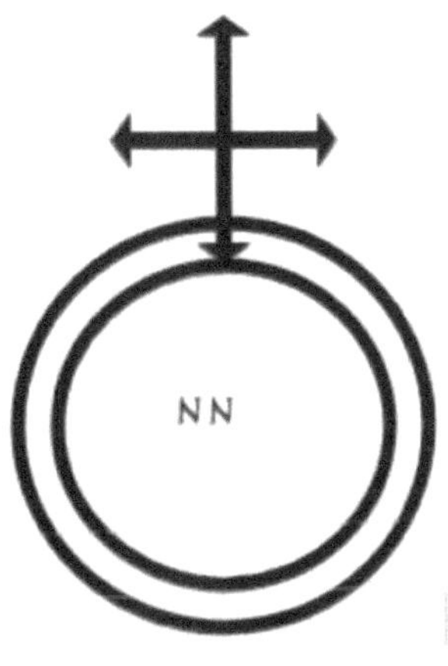

-Oraison-

"Oh glorious name of the Great and Living God who in all times and in all things is present, I who am your servant (your name) Eternal Father beseech you to send your Angels whose names are written in the Holy Circle to show themselves to me and that which I am eager to know and to learn. In the name of Our Lord and Savior Jesus Christ, let this be so."

To make a snake freeze

Make a solution of alum then take a bit of paper and write upon it in goat's blood: *"Halt oh supple one, for here is a pledge."* Soak the paper in the alum solution and throw it at the snake. Now take a wicker wand and move it through the air such that it whistles. If the wand touches the snake it will die or flee immediately.

To stop a horse or team of horses.

Trace the sign of Beelzebub on some black paper with white ink and throw it at the head of the lead horse in a team saying: "White horse or black, whatever color ye be, it is I who command you not to lift a hooves as you lift your ears, and none but **Beelzebub** can break this bond." For this spell you should have a nail forged during midnight mass that you can throw before the horse's face. For three days before you cast this spell you should take care to avoid good Christian deeds.

For Invisibility.

You must steal a black cat and then buy a new terracotta pot without haggling. Obtain a magic mirror, a burning taper, some charcoal and some tinder that you will keep on your person. Go to a fountain at midnight and collect some water, then light your fire. Put the cat in the pot and the pot on the flame. Hold the cover in your left hand without moving it or looking behind you when you hear a noise. After boiling the cat for 24 hours you must place it on a new plate. Remove the bones and throw the flesh over your left shoulder while saying: "Accipe quod tibi do, et nihil amplius." Place the bones between your teeth one by one with your left hand while looking in the mirror to see if you have vanished. If you don't disappear when all of the bones are in, throw them away over your left shoulder one by one until the spell is cast. Once you cannot see yourself in the mirror, withdraw saying: "*Pater in manus tuas commendo spiritum meum. Keep these bones from the eyes of the profane.*" After that becoming invisible is merely a matter placing the bones between your teeth.

To win at games

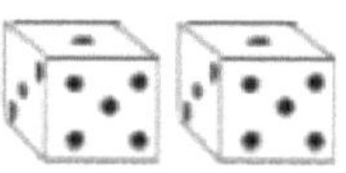

Take a four or five leaf clover which was gathered during a thunderstorm. Make the sign of the cross over it and say: "Clover I picked you in the Name of the Father, the Son and the Holy Ghost, and by the Virginity of the Blessed Virgin and of Saint John the Evangelist, and you will serve me in all games of chance." Now say five *Our Fathers* and five *Hail Marys* before continuing: "El, Agios, Ischiros, Atanathos." Enclose this clover in a black silken bag that you must wear about with you whenever you gamble. When not in use you should keep it safe.

-NATURAL MAGIC-

The traditions of all peoples give us a vast number of spell to employ in order to attract love or to be rid of importunate passions. The results obtained can be turned on oneself or aimed at a third party.

The greatest single agent of magical operations is the Will. The Will puts at our disposal a means of action which is commonly referred to as **BAPHOMET**.

Ardent intention is enough to work all sorts of marvels. The All Powerful Name in magic pertaining to love is **SHEVAH.**

To awaken love you must turn to rites that make use of gold, ambergris, chives, periwinkle, verbena, wormwood, St. John's

Wort, the genitals of a hare, a dove, a sparrow, a goat, the hippomane, human blood and semen, etc.

To impart strength for copulation, infuse some knotweed, verbena, henbane, and fennel juice into milk, incense, myrrh, musk, the tops of savory plants, coriander, etc.

The Arab magicians make use of magnetism applied to the cerebro-spinal matrix, the solar plexus, the genitals and the lungs by means of a very long, fine quill. This procedure is very effective if there be love between two spouses.

There are other more agreeable practices that come to us from our Celtic forefathers and can be of use to curious young women. This it is good to spread such practices.

That which the vulgar call the "secrets of love" have two distinct goals. In the first category we have all of those operations that have for their object to directly awaken either love or hatred in the heart of another person.

In the second category we have all of those operations achieved through either a mental or external apparition.

In order to gain the love of a person you must write upon a piece of virgin parchment the following words:

"Sator, Arepo, Tenet, Opera, Rotas, Jah, Jah, Jah, Enam, Jah, Jah, Ketler, Chokmah, Rinah, Tedulah, Teburah, Tiphereth, Netzah, Hod, Jesod, Malkouth, Abraham, Isaac, Jacob, Shadrach, Meshach, Abednego, come to aid in all that I desire."

At this point it is enough to get the beloved to accept an object of any kind.

Here is a formula much used in Bengal:

If a woman wants her husband to love her more fully she will fill a glass with some magnetized water. After blowing on the water seventy times she has her husband drink the water under some pretext or another. This process must be repeated five times.

The gift a girl can give to keep her fiance's love forever.

Take three hairs from your head, roll them together into a tight little ball and place three drops of blood from your left ring finger onto the ball. Wear this talisman against your bosom without telling a soul for 9 days and 9 nights, then hide the ball in a ring or broach and present it to your lover. While he wears the ornament his heart belongs to you and you alone.

Take a long lock of your hair and mingle it with the hair of a goat. Douse the whole in some lamp oil and it shall have the same effect, but you must keep the secret of this operation for all of your days, even from your closest friends, or it will destroy marital happiness.

To find out if you are beloved by A certain person.

Take an apple and slice it in two with a very sharp knife. If you can do this without cutting a seed you are beloved, but should you by chance cut into a seed you have not won the person's heart.

To know if you are loved in general.

Choose a Friday, curious girl, preferably the Friday of a waxing moon, or better still when the moon is in the sign of *Taurus* or *Libra*. On the chosen day you shall take a morning bath before going into the garden to gather a handful of marjolaine, thyme, and bengal roses. Hide these in your room and let them dry for seven days. On the following Friday crush the plants into a fine powder with great care and without hurry.

Now take double that amount of barley flour and with the powder make a cake by adding the milk of a roan cow that is young and fit.

Do not cook this cake but wrap it up in a fresh white sheet of paper and place it beneath the head of your bed. At night sleep with your head on the right side above the cake.

Be sure the paper you use be clean. If you dream of music, parties, and all of the things of **Venus**, then your heart's desire shall be fulfilled soon.

To dream of the man you will marry, keep your window open on the Eve of Saint Andrew and take the apple someone sets there without thanking them. Cut the fruit in twain and eat one half before midnight and the other half after midnight. Now sleep, and in dreams you shall see your future husband.

Or indeed you could go and pluck a leaf of ivy at bedtime and place it under your pillow without looking at it, and you shall dream of the one you love.

Here is a very effective secret: Once you know it you should keep it to yourself. Choose a feast day and get up at night eight hours before the rising of the sun. Make sure nobody sees you as you run to the garden to pluck a laurel branch. Return to your room where you shall have prepared a pot with some sulfur. Light the fire and wave your laurel wand over the sulfurous smoke as you count from 1 to 365 which is the mystical number of a certain Angel of great power. Now wrap your magic wand in some white linen followed by some white paper that you will have purchased expressly for this operation, upon which you will have written your name and the name of your lover or lovers if you have several. Add the name of the day and its number within the month upon which you perform the spell, along with the hour and the current phase of the moon and the dominant planet. Now bury this packet in a secret place. Unearth it at the end of 3 days and 3 nights, place it beneath your pillow for the 3 following nights, and you shall come to know the spouse Heaven has chosen for you.

Here is another secret: On the three days following the feast of Saint John you should go to the garden and examine the roses there. Choose one that is deep red and which seems sure to wilt by the third day, but you must only look upon it and never touch it. On the morning of the fourth day rise with the sun and, taking care that no one sees you, go forth and cut the rose and bring it to your room. There you shall have a pot with a bit of sulfur in it. Expose the flower to the fumes of the sulfur until it has changed color entirely. Now fold it up in some paper provided for the purpose upon which you shall write your name, the name of your best friend, the date and day of the month, the year, the phase of the moon and the name of the dominant zodiac sign and planet. Fold the paper thrice and bury the packet at the foot of a tree, and from there pluck another flower which you will wear on your person for nine days. On the ninth day dig up your package, go to bed, and sleep with your head above the talisman. You shall dream dreams of great import for three days, as the flower will have magical virtue during that time.

Here is another, simpler ritual. Choose the night of the first full moon of the year. Work extra hard on this day and wear yourself out a bit more than usual. After the evening meal go and wash your hands, mouth and eyes, and anoint your hair and head with several drops of water. Now go forth to a place that is well removed, to the gate at the edge of a field for example, and lean upon the bar that holds the gate shut. Look at the moon and say:

> "Salut ! Moon I salute thee !
> This night oh moon, make plain
> The man who'll marry me !"

Now salute the moon again very quietly and return home to sleep in silence. If your heart be firm, you will certainly dream of your future husband.

You can also call upon the help of St. Peter. In order to do so you must choose the night before his feast day and gather up nine keys. It is best if you procure these keys without borrowing them due to the secrecy that must be maintained in these matters. Wind a lock of your hair into three braids. Now, from each of the ends of the three locks of hair which form the threefold braid you shall hang three keys and knot your hair such that the keys hang there. Tie all of these to your left wrist using the garter from you left leg and tie your right garter around your forehead.

Just before going to sleep speak the following incantation with passion:

"*Saint Peter be not angry with us. I have cast this spell to gain your favor. You who are the Lord of Keys grant me my wish, I pray you, and give me proof of your power. Make it such that I may see my future lover and spouse, Amen.*"

Here are some simple auguries which will indicate what your conjugal future might hold:

On the feast of Saint Sylvester you should throw your left shoe into the branches of a hornbeam tree. If your shoe remains in the tree you will be married within the year. If you throw the shoe nine times and it falls back every time, several years will pass before you find yourself at the altar.

Another secret: Take two lengths of ribbon of the same quality and the color of a pigeon's neck. Fold them in half for greater efficacy and tie the two together at the midpoint with a bit of silk of the same color. To this bit of silk attach a buckle borrowed from a friend. Take a tie-pin from your beloved without telling him what it is for and hang it outside of your window. Attach the bundle of ribbon to the tie-pin and attach the four ends of this talisman to the wall with pins in the form of a cross. The wall must be exposed to the sunlight and you must not look at the ribbons. Do not touch the talisman for three hours. If at the end of this period the color has changed you will not marry your current lover. If the ribbons maintain their color you will marry soon and be very happy.

Here are some tricks through which ordinary card games can reveal who among your young friends will someday be your husband. Invite 2, 4, or 6 of your friends, throw a deck of cards into a canvas sack and shake it. Pass the sack around so that everyone can give it a shake without touching the cards. Once this is done the sack is passed in the inverse direction with each person taking one card without looking at it. Now show the cards to one another. Whoever draws the high card will be married first be she young, old, or a widow. Whoever draws the low card will surely marry last.

If you wish to know the age of your spouse-to-be take nine seeds from the thornapple that the scholars call datura stramonium and nine pinches of freshly turned earth from nine different parts of a field along with water from a newfound spring or a reservoir. Make a cake of all of this and set it on the ground at a crossroads at sunrise on Easter or the feast of Saint Michael. Hide yourself and watch to see who first treads upon the cake. If it be a woman your husband will be old or a widower, if it be a man your husband will be young.

The daughters of fishermen perform the following ceremony to discover their destiny in such matters. At midnight on New Year's or the feast of Saint George they go to a crossroads at midnight with a bottle of eau-de-vie and some fried fish. There they sit upon the ground placing the bottle and the fish before them, then wait in silence.

The image of their husband-to-be appears slowly, and if he takes the fish the marriage will be a happy one. If he takes the liquor the marriage will be a misfortune.

If you wish to discover your future status, choose a Saturday or Sunday night closest to the feast of Saint Leon. Take a hazelnut and a nutmeg pod and crush them into powder before making nine little pills by adding the mix to some butter that you will have made yourself. Eat the nine pills before going to bed and your dreams will reveal the status of the man you will marry. If you dream of riches you will marry a nobleman or a man of means, if you dream of night you will marry a lawyer, and if you hear a tumult your will marry a businessman. If your husband is to be a soldier or a sailor you shall dream of thunder and lightning, and if he is to be a servant you will dream of rain.

Here are some other signs belonging to the science that the ancients called **ornithomancy.**

If while walking you see a single magpie it is a bad omen, above all if it flies before you and to the left. If it flies on your right it is a good sign. If you see two magpies it means you will soon receive a good offer for marriage or an inheritance. If the magpies fly off on your right it means that your marriage or that of a person close to you will soon come to pass.

The love letters you receive from your lover can be used to test his true intentions without him knowing it. When you receive a letter from him wherein he professes his love, place the open letter on the table and gaze at it while counting in a low voice to seventy-two. Now fold the letter three times from top to bottom. Pin the folded letter to your corsage and place it over your heart. Leave it there until bedtime, and when you lay down rest it on your head. If you dream of weeping or your lover salutes you you should be rid of him, he's a fraud. If you dream of precious stones he is a faithful man who will keep his promises. If you dream of white linen you will be a widow.

Here is a curious phenomenon: Rise with the sun on the 14th of February which is the day of Saint Valentine and immediately make a bouquet of yellow crocuses. The first man who enters your house will be your future husband or at the very least the two of you will have the same last name.

Or again on this same morning gather five laurel leaves. Pin one to each corner of your pillow and put the last in the middle. Before going to sleep repeat the following prayer seven times: *"Oh great Saint Valentine protector of lovers, make it such that I will soon see the one who will be my faithful and tender companion."*

You can discover the family name of your future spouse or a friend's. Take a small Bible and open it to chapter VII verses 6 and 7 of the ***Song of Solomon***. Take the key to your door and place it on this page at the level of these verses. Close the book with the key inside and bind it tightly with your left garter. If you are alone you should suspend the book in the air from your left pinky finger. If you are with a friend make it so that you can both hold it. Read the verses aloud and then commence to recite the alphabet slowly. The Bible will move when you pronounce the first letter of your future husband's last name.

If you are a boy or a girl, if you are in love and you find a piece of red cloth on the ground, especially wool, pick it up immediately and make a wish for good fortune in love. To find love wear the cloth about as an amulet.

Your wish will come true even if your beloved has no affection for you, just make your wish for such-and-such a person.

If a young man can procure the shoe of his beloved he should wear it over his heart constantly. If he hangs it at the head of his bed decked with some rue leaves he will be sure to find prompt success in love.

Here is a practice that comes down to us from the Druids: It is for seeing the apparition of the future spouses of three young ladies. Make a garland of juniper and mistletoe a bit longer than three feet and bind yourself to two other maidens. Mistletoe from an oak tree works the best. Cast the spell on a Wednesday or a Friday near Christmas. Place acorns at even intervals along the garland, and make it such that you will be alone around midnight. Close and lock the door and hang the key over the fireplace after you have a good fire going. Open the window. All three of you must remain silent. You should have a slat of wood some two and one half feet long. Twist the garland around the wood, working together. Throw the garland wrapped wood on the flames and step back in silence setting your left knee on the floor. Each girl should hold her mass book open to the page containing wedding rites. When the last acorn is consumed by the fire each girl will see her groom-to-be. If one of the girls should see a coffin or something of that kind it means she will not marry. Now go to bed where further revelations await you in dreams.

Another means of conjuring the image of your future husband is available, but there is some danger, above all if you do not follow the instructions provided to the letter.

On a Friday night preceding the Sunday of Quasimodo, go alone and unseen to a crossroads in the countryside. Once there let your hair down and let it hang behind you as did the Celtic prophetesses of yore. You shall have taken a pin with you that has never been used with which you will prick the little finger of your left hand. Let fall 3 drops of blood upon the ground and repeat with each drop: "I give my blood to the one I love that I may see he and he shall be mine." The image of your husband will arise from the drops of blood only to vanish immediately when fully formed. Take up the bit of mud formed by your blood and turn to the east, north, west and south, letting a bit of mud fall over your left shoulder with each stop while intoning: "Spirits go back to your domains, in the name of the Father Almighty." Then you must make a novena at the altar of the Virgin to honor the Elemental Spirits. If you forget to do any of these things a terrible, perhaps mortal misfortune will befall you within the year.

There is still another secret for obtaining the same information. Find a number of young maidens to assist you and give them the wherewithal to make a cake with flour, apples, nine thornapple seeds, some ash, verbena, and the milk of a cow that has only given birth once. They must bake the cake on a Friday on the 13th day of the lunar month between eleven and midnight. Let each of them trace their individual portions into the cake with their hair pins, and each shall inscribe their portion with the first three letters of their names. Let them place the cake before the fire and sit in silence along the walls of the room watching the cake after each has turned the cake around three times. Upon the twelfth stroke of midnight they shall see the form of a man traversing the room to put his hand on the cake. The portion of the cake touched by the phantom will indicate the name of the girl who will marry first.

People know many spells for punishing a lover who strays and for **knotting the cord** in various ways to force someone to love them. I do not wish to provide any of these: The ingeniousness of malevolent people is rather great, and it is better to pardon an offense than to seek an eye for an eye.

Moreover the candle, the taper, the heart of the calf and the pins, the flowers and roots, the hair from a horse's belly, etc., are well known procedures.

When conversing with a young lady that you wish to gain the affection of, you can pretend you want to cast her horoscope, for example, if she is soon to be married. In this interview, which should take place in private, try to get her to look you in the face and, when your gazes meet, say resolutely: "*Kaphe, Kasita, non Kapheta et publica filii omnibus suis.*" Do not be astonished by this enigmatic language the occult meaning of which you do not grasp, and if you say it with faith, you shall be loved.

Draw some of your blood on a Friday in the Spring and let it dry in a little pot with two rabbit pellets and the liver of a dove. Crush it all into a powder and find a way to make the object of your love ingest this, the quantity needed being about one half of a gram. If this has not effect the first time try again up to three times, and you shall be loved.

Take a bit of virgin parchment and write the words: "*Michael, Gabriel, Raphael, make this person (name her) conceive a love for me equal to my own.*" Now find way to attach this to the headboard of her bed as close to where her pillow is as possible. Soon she will not be able to sleep because she will be thinking of you.

To keep a lover faithful take a lock of their hair and burn it. Spread the ash on the wooden frame of their bed with some honey. They will think of no one but you. It is easy enough to renew this elixir from time to time to keep love constant.

Do you wish your love letters to have the desired effect? Take a sheet of virgin parchment and cover both sides with the following words: "*Adam, Evah. As the Almighty Creator unites us in terrestrial paradise with a sacred bond which is mutual and unbreakable, let the heart of the one I adore be ever favorable to me: Ely+ Ely+ Ely+.*" Burn the parchment and gather the ash with care. Take some fresh ink and pour it into a new little terracotta pot. Mix in the ash and seven drops of milk from a woman nursing her first born and add a pinch of filings from a magnet. Sharpen a new quill with a new penknife. Every person you write to using this equipment will fall under your spell.

Take five of your hairs and twist them up with five hairs from your beloved, then throw them in the fire saying: "*Ure, igne Sancti Spiritus, renes nestros et cor nostrum, Domine Spiritus, Amen.*" Your love will bear fruit.

On the eve of Saint John before the rising of the sun go and gather the plant called **Oenula Campana.** Carry in clean linen over your heart for nine days and then crush it into a powder. Now sprinkle on a bouquet or a cake that you present to your beloved, and they will be yours.

Pour some white lily oil into a crystal cup and recite the 137th psalm over this. When you finish pronounce the word "**Anaël**" and the name of your beloved. Write the name on a bit of cypress wood and plunge it in oil. Anoint your eyelids lightly with the oil and tie the bit of cypress to your right arm. Now look for the right moment to touch your beloved with your right hand at which point the flame of love will be kindled. The spell is more powerful if you perform it at sunrise on the Friday following a new moon.

Have a golden ring set with a little diamond that has never been used for anything else since it was taken from the earth. Wrap this in some silken cloth and carry it with you for 9 days and 9 nights between your shirt and your skin against your heart. On the ninth day before sunrise etch the word "**Shevah**" into the ring. Now take a few hairs pilfered from the object of your love and twist them up with several of your own while saying: "Oh body, see fit to love me, and let me find success through the power of Shevah." Wrap the ring up in the hairs and place it in the silken bag, then carry this talisman around for another 6 days. On the 7th day take the ring out and make it ready so that you may give it to your beloved upon their arrival. This should all be done before the rising of the sun and while fasting.

For Love

On the 1st Friday of the moon buy half an ell of red ribbon in the name of your beloved. Tie a figure 8 knot but don't pull it taut, but say the prayer "Pater... in tentationem..." and replace "seb libera nos a malo" with "ludea-ludei-ludeo." As you pronounce these words pull the ribbon taut.

Add one *Pater* each day until you reach the ninth day and add a knot each day. Wrap the ribbon around your left arm and touch the object of your desire with this hand.

He-goat.

Mix some billy-goat droppings with a quantity of wheat flour and dry the mixture, then make little pills and heat these up in some oil. Rub some of this on your foreskin when you are ready to make love and afterward your lady will be incapable of loving anyone but you.

You can obtain the same effect with goat fat.

How you can dream of the one you are destined to marry.

If a man should wish to dream of the woman he shall marry he must obtain some crushed coral, some shavings from a magnet, a bit of dough and the blood of a white pigeon. Mix the lot and stuff it into a large fig after having folded it up in a square of blue silk. Wear this around your neck and place a myrtle branch on your bedside table, intoning: "Kyrie clementissime, qui Abraham servo tuo dedistis uxorem et filio ejus obedientissimo per admirabile signum indicasti Rebeccam uxorem, indica mihi servo tuo quam nupturus sim uxorem per mysterium tuorum Spirituum Baalibeth, Assaibi, Abumostith men, Amen."

In the morning you must recall to mind the images you saw in dreams. If you saw nothing you must repeat the spell on the three following Fridays and, if you do not see any image after this time, it means you will not be married.

If a girl should desire to see the man she will wed in dreams she must take a little poplar branch and tie it to her arm with a white ribbon. Now all of this must be removed and placed under the bedside table. Sprinkle your temples with the blood of the hoopoe bird before going to bed and reciting the oraison mentioned above before sleeping.

To draw a girl to you no matter how prudent she may be.

If the moon is just waxing or toward the end of its waning you should look up and pick out a star between the hours of eleven and midnight. Now do the following: Take some virgin parchment cut into the form of a circle with a cross projecting from the top and write the name of your beloved upon it. The name of your beloved goes in the center of the circle, and then you must turn the parchment over and write the following names: Machidael, Barofchas. Put your parchment on the ground with the person's name facing down. Put your right foot on the parchment and your left knee on the ground beside it. Now look up at your chosen star and hold forth a white candle in your right hand which will be able to burn for one hour. Say the following conjuration:

"I salute and conjure you oh lovely moon and beautiful star, brilliant light that I take in my hand by the air that I breathe and which is in me and by the earth I touch. I conjure you in the names of the spirits, the princes who preside over you, and the ineffable name of the one who created all, by you beautiful Gabriel and Prince Mercury, Michael, and Melchidael. I conjure you again by all of the divine names of God that you should obsess and torment the body, mind, and soul of Y whose name is written here, such that she must run to me (speak your name) and do my will and want no other in the world save me, X, even though she now be indifferent toward me. Let it be unendurable, let her be obsessed, let her suffer and be tormented. Go then promptly oh Melchidael, Bareschas, Zazel, Tiriel, Malcha and all of those who are among you. I conjure you by the Great and living God to go forth and do my will. I, **X**, promise to satisfy you."

Be sure to specify the day upon which you wish your beloved to be driven into your arms and she will come without question.

To prevent copulation

For this spell you must have a new pencil. Then on a Saturday at the exact hour of the rising of the moon you shall retrieve the parchment which you will have kept for a time affixed to the back of a bedroom door. Upon this trace the following figures and the words **Consumatum est** before breaking the pencil lead off in the door.

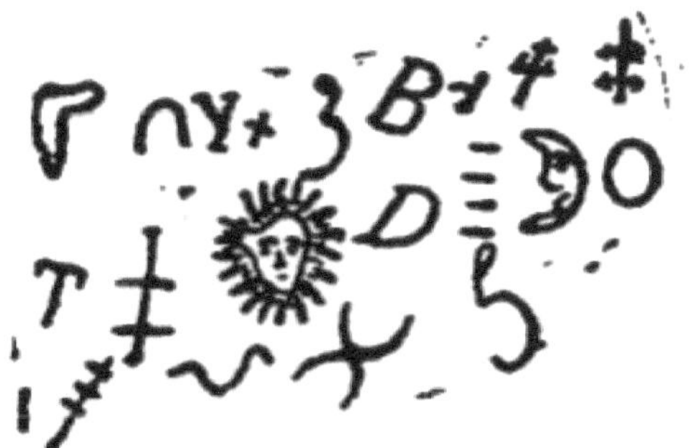

The ancient ones assure us that the bird we call the *woodpecker* is a perfect defense against the infertility spell we call the **knotted cord** if it be eaten roasted after a fasting period with some blessed salt. If you inhale the smoke from the burning tooth of a man who has recently died you will also be delivered from the spell.

The same effect is achieved if you put some quicksilver in a blowpipe made from oat straw and place this talisman beneath the bed of the enchanted individual. If a man and a woman cannot conceive because of this spell, the man must urinate through his wedding ring while the wife holds it.

To reconcile those separated by questions of personal interest.

If you wish to bring concord among your friends and allies who are divided for the moment, walk around your town three times in a clockwise fashion while carrying a sandstone vase containing water and soft butter. Pour the water out in the public square and have the feuding parties eat the butter as well as portions of grilled meat from a three year old heifer. This same ceremony should be performed for another three days, and on each day both parties should be provided with various foods and drinks. Do this with a great desire for peace in your heart.

Steal a Cow's milk

Take for pieces of wheat straw from this year's harvest and have it blessed on the day of the Dead (hiding the true cause for the benediction from the Priest, of course). Go to the gates of a cemetery at midnight during the waning of the moon and evoque the soul of one who died without the sacrament of confession, begging them to come to your aid and go with this restless spirit to the stalls where the cows are waiting. On the doorstep place two straws in the form of a cross. Keep the other two, and on the next day at the hour of Saturn or of Mars mix them into the feed of those cows which you would render dry. When performed on the 18th the spell always works.

To restore milk to cows.

On a night of the new moon when evening comes on you must make a cake of oats and pronounce the *exorcism of water* over it five times, each time adding a few drops of holy water to the cake. Keep a handful of the cake and feed the rest to the cattle. After this you should bind the cows together by means of a string passed around the left horn of each. Now make three turns around the stable in a counter-clockwise direction while reciting the **conjuration of the four.** When you are finished you will see the one who cast the evil spell upon the cows, as the person will be drawn there by an irresistible urge. Throw you remaining bit of the oat-cake into the person's face and command them to lift the spell at once, and they will obey or be frozen on the spot indefinitely and unable to free themselves.

A Hindu Amulet

To forge an excellent talisman enclose a pinch of earth from an ant mound and a bit of turf in a bag made from the skin of a stillborn goat. Add a tuft of elephant hair and a piece of ivory.

A means of divination in various Embarrassing situations.

Take a blessed rice cooker and a blessed vase and recite the magical oraison of the day. When finished close your eyes and turn toward the sun pronouncing one of these two phrases: "It is cooked." or "It is not cooked." Now look at the rice cooker and if your spell has been successful the solution within will show the outcome you desire.

Another means

On the day and at the hour of the sun you can take a fistful of wheat straw into a field and say while intoning the word "odd" or "even" repeatedly. The desired end will arrive.

Yet another means.

Say "odd" or "even" while forming a heap of 21 stones from a quantity held in your left hand. Balance a cane atop this pile and see if you can guess whether it falls to the left or the right.

Choice of a husband.

In the open air stretch out a white cloth the four corners of which shall face the cardinal compass points. The young lady looking to be wed shall place a handful of blessed seeds at each corner while reciting the exorcism of the air.

Choice of a wife.

Take 3 clods of earth taken from an anthill, a crossroads, and a cemetery. Recite the oraison of the gnomes while waving your hands over these. Have the girl you love come and choose one of the clumps of earth. If she chooses the anthill she will be a good wife and partner. If she choose the crossroads she will be flighty. If she choose the cemetery she will die before giving birth.

Another means

Take a vase of water blessed by the oraison of the undines and ask your beloved to plunge her hand into it hard enough to cause some spillage. If the water falls to the east it is a sign that you shall be happily married to her.

To bring back a fiance who has been lured
Away by another woman.

Make a satchel with the skin of a cow killed on a farm where a death has recently occurred. Put some object owned by your rival into the satchel and smash them to powder (insofar as possible.) Bury this in front of her door with three stones set over it.

Another means

Take some of your rival's hair and form three little rings with it which you then attach to a black silken thread. Now dig a hole and bury either a ring or a stone while cursing the other woman. Your rival can break the spell if she finds the hole and says over it: "If someone sought to bury my joy under three stones, I now break the spell and profit thereby."

To kindle love in the young lady
That you wish to marry.

Place twenty-one thorny twigs on the fire with the spines facing east and twenty-one jujube branches attached with a red thread. Now, three times per day for the next three days you must warm some elderberry branches dipped in butter by this fire.

At night you should turn your bed upside down and hang a pot of hot water over it suspended by three new threads. Lay on you inverted bed and swing the pot by pushing it with your toes.

In this ritual we find various symbols: The fire is for passion, the color red is for love, the plants are all consecrated to **Venus,** and the inverted bed indicates that one does not sleep on the wedding night but makes love. The pot of water represents the young woman's heart which palpitates ceaselessly.

To be sure the planting goes well

On the night before you sow seed in the field take some dirt from an anthill, some sod, some sand, and some seeds for those trees sacred to *Jupiter* and **Mercury**. Place all of this in a sack suspended from a tripod the legs of which are made from jujube branches.

After this make a good meal and place the leftovers in the sack.

On the next day when the sowing is to occur, bury this sack in the center of the field. Have a handful of oat seeds that have been dipped in blessed pork-fat and throw some toward the cardinal compass points as you turn about three times.

An amulet to lend you vital energy

A very effective amulet can be made from the genital hair of the males of seven different types: A lion, a tiger, a goat, a ram, a bull, a warrior, and a king.

To turn the course of a disputed stream or one that is needed elsewhere

Dig a furrow that is one foot wide and recite the ***oraison of the gnomes.*** Stand astride the furrow and pour some blessed water into it. Throw two pieces of gold into the furrow and cover it using stems of bamboo placed lengthwise along it, returning the next day to remove them.

To know if your herds will prosper

Go far into the countryside on the *Day of the Sun* (see *Kabbalistic Astrology*) at an hour when you still do not hear any sounds from the fields and turn toward the four cardinal compass points calling out three times in a loud voice to the Angel who rules the wind from each direction.

If the first animal you hear is neither a donkey or a dog it will be a good year for your flocks. If you hear a donkey bray or a dog bark the omen is indeed bad.

To grant intelligence to a newborn

When the child is born the father should breath thrice upon his forehead and place upon his tongue a pill made from butter, honey, and blessed milk.

To protect a field from rats, moles, field mice & other destructive pests

Walk three times around a field in a clockwise direction while reciting the ***oraison of the gnomes*** (see Magical Traditions) while sowing some iron filings and fine sand that you mix in your hands and allow to pour from between your fingers. After this take a mole whose snout is bound shut with black horsehair and throw it into the middle of the field. At this point you should stay in the field and work, but refrain from saying a single word until sundown.

Regain a lost object

Spend a full night in room in the center of which has been set a pot of holy water. Have two maidens who have never menstruated and who do not know the room come in. Have them turn around twice in place and tell them to carry the pot off to some other place. The side toward which they carry the pot shows you where to begin searching for your lost item.

To restore peace in a village

A sorcerer should walk thrice around the village on the day and at the hour of **Venus** such that his right hand is always facing town. He shall carry a pitcher of holy water (see Magical Tradition) on his shoulder and at the end of his circumambulation he shall pour it out on the town square.

To bring a lost dog home

Go to a field at noon and place four stones in a square such that each corner faces a cardinal compass point. On the north point burn some cedar, on the east point burn some ashwood, on the south point burn some pine, and on the west point burn some rosewood. Stand in the center of these and recite the ***Conjuration of the Four***. Gather up the ashes of the four different woods into four silken bags. When night comes down and the moon has risen go about tossing a pinch of each kind of ash in various places around the house. If this does not meet with success, try the same operation again in three days, and on the fourth morning your dog will be at your door.

Against slander

If you hear talk about you that is calumnious, eat three oatcakes dipped in blessed milk and spread dried and crushed leaves of verbena around your home.

To break a fever

Attach a frog to the foot of the sick person's bed with a red and black string. Wash the patient with holy water and squeeze the cloth over the frog such that the water falls onto him. When this is done chase the frog from the room.

Another means

Have the patient drink some water in which you have boiled black rice heated over coals taken from a forest fire, then place a few of the rice grains on his forehead.

Keep chickens from laying

On the day and at the hour **Saturn** take five turns around the victim's farm in a counterclockwise direction. Every thirty paces you should stop and throw some magnet shavings in the direction of the henhouse.

Once you have made your last turn around the farm the chickens will find a way out of the coop and they will run toward the magician. Throw them a handful of meal that has been lightly toasted. The chickens will return to the coop where the rooster waits, but he will be unable to cover them for three months, and so they shall have no chicks.

Against migraines

Have the afflicted person lay down on a couch or sofa such that his head is to the north and his feet are to the south. Lightly caress his forehead from the middle to the temples with the feather of a red ibis. Halt every three minutes to speak the **Conjuration of the Four** while holding by turns the head, feet, right side and left side of the patient. After repeating this ceremony seven times the operator finishes by calling upon the Angel of the wind that prevails that day (see Kabbalistic Astrology) while facing the direction from which the wind blows.

Fertile cows.

Circle the herd three times in a clockwise manner while anointing the animals with an elderberry branch dipped in Holy Water (see Magical Tradition, 3rd part on Spells).

Another means

Take some milk from a cow that has just calved (provided the calf produced is the same color as its mother!) and mingle this same cow's saliva with some bull droppings. Heat this mixture before a fire on the first three days after the new moon. On the thirteenth day clean the stable and anoint it with holy water. Now take some dung from each cow and place it in a heap in the midst of the stable. Throw some of the mixture described above into every corner of the stable while standing on the dung pile at the center.

To guard against snakes & vermin

Trace a circle three times around the area to be protected, be it a field or a house, moving from right to left. Take whatever you find in the rumen of a cow or the belly of a fresh-killed goat and spread some of this substance on the ground or in the house before throwing the rest on the fire. Now bury several plants consecrated to **Saturn** with the stem in the ground and the roots in the air.

To win a young lady's love

Touch her with a paste composed of a magical unguent made from the juice of the herbs of **Venus** (see Kabbalistic Astrology, herbs of Venus) some licorice, and a bit of turf crushed between two slices of wood taken from a tree with vines covering its trunk.

To avoid the tricks of a femme fatale

When you fear the temptations of a woman whose love you feel will surely lead you into ruin you should take some soil from the place where a black goat treads and place it in a satchel made from a toad's skin dried in the sun. Keep this talisman in a room for three days with the shutters closed.

On the day at at the hour of **Saturn** you should plunge your left thumb into this dirt and use it to mark your forehead, eyelids, chin, palms, and the soles of your feet.

Take the rest of the dirt and throw it against the woman's front door, then turn and go home without looking back.

To calm jealousy

Plunge a red hot poker into some holy water and have the jealous person drink the water while it is still warm.

For the successful delivery of a baby

In the north of Germany when a woman is about to give birth all of the windows and drawers in the home are opened wide, then lunar plants gathered at sunset are wound up in the mother's hair. In India the Brahmins will untie all of the knots in a house when it is time for a woman to give birth.

To be rid of a curse brought upon your home

By some enchanted object

Attach the left foot of a crow or raven to the object you believe to be cursed, then let the bird fly off at midnight on the first day of the full moon.

Against infected glands

Make a pile with some twigs from a walnut tree and set it afire while reciting the **exorcism of flame** (see Magical Tradition). Pass some paracu leaves through the flame and extract the juice of the leaves, gathering it in the bottom of a broken bottle. Take some of this mixture in a wooden spoon you yourself have carved and pour it on the swollen gland. On the next day take some shells you have gathered at low tide and crush them on the while seated by side of your house that faces the setting sun. Rub the boil with this powder and place a leech upon it. On the third day rub the gland with a dog's saliva. Cut the tail from a lizard and have the animal bite the swollen node, then set it free immediately.

To put everyone to sleep in the house

<h1 style="text-align:center;">where the object of your love resides</h1>

Recite a sleep incantation while gazing at the house of your beloved and concentrating your will. Think entirely of the house where her parents keep watch making life impossible for you.

Anoint the house with holy water and pour some under the crack of the front door, then sprinkle the front door itself with the juice of a poppy cut on the day and at the hour of **Venus** (see the "Magic Clock" in the book "Spells").

To triumph over a rival

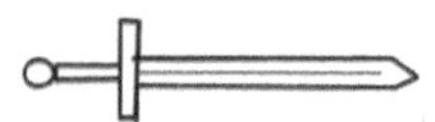

A woman who wants to drive off a rival should procure some milk from a black goat. She should then pour out some water and throw some eucalyptus leaves which have been resting on her bed upon said water. The remainder of the leaves should be boiled in the black goat's milk and the resulting liquid is then poured in a circle around the bed.

To assure the fidelity of two lovers who

Are separated by a long voyage

Have them both wear a bracelet on the left wrist made from the stem of the plant that the Hindus call the *Sauvarcala*. The plant has a strong odor, it causes the eyes to tear, and it has aphrodisiac qualities. The root of this plant, like the mandrake, generally takes on a humanoid form.

To reconcile adversaries

The Hindus prescribe having one of the adversaries string a bow while standing in the other's shadow. Another rite includes getting the party who craves reconciliation to carry a stone with him, set it down, and have both parties spit upon it. The stone thus represents the foundation of a new friendship, and this is what the sacred books of the Vedas term "burying anger."

To staunch the blood from wounds

Pour some lacquer gum into boiling water. Filter the mixture and mix it with some warm milk. The wounded person should drink this as hot as he can stand it.

On the following night at the hour when the stars begin to fade pour the lacquer mixture into some water and heat it up, then soak it into some cloth and apply this to the wound.

When morning comes dab the wound with butter mixed into milk, and what remains should be consumed by the patient.

To be rid of any obsession

To escape the condition of obsession by a wicked spirit or by some person using black magic during the new moon, you must wait for the first day of the full moon (a clear night is necessary) and go to the banks of some flowing river, creek or stream at a point where it makes a quick turn toward the south. Come dressed in black vestments. You shall have made a raft which you will have made fast to the riverbank and which you will now climb onto. Make a fire on the raft using some straw taken from a thatched roof, and over this you must bake a pancake sprinkled with a mix of corn and manioc flour. After this climb off of the raft, dismantle it, and bury the pieces. Throw your black vestments into the water and put on new clothes along with shoes made from the skin of an animal that was killed (and did not die from age or disease). Return home without looking behind you.

To exorcise a haunted house

Throw some cypress logs cut from a live tree onto the fire on the day and at the hour of **Saturn.** Perform a fumigation with the smoke, then take some stakes made of thuya wood and drive them fully into the ground around the house. You shall have some small stones taken from a riverbed at midnight in bare feet. Take these and put them into the fire until they glow, then place one of them in every room of the house.

To turn a curse cast on a field
Back upon the magician

Sprinkle the perimeter of the cursed field with some holy water and draw a triangle in the midst of the field the sides of which should measure ten feet. Mark the corner angles with white stones taken from a cemetery, then plow the interior of the triangle with a plow drawn by two black bulls.

Against hereditary illness

Attach some amaryllis branches to the arms and legs of the patient and lead them to a crossroads before removing the twigs and putting these into a sack. This sack, which shall have been made from the skin of a slaughtered animal, is now worn about the neck.

Against partial paralysis

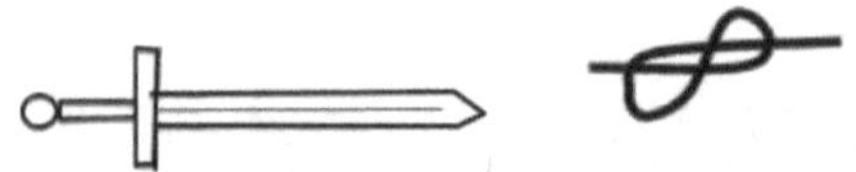

Seek the footprints of a large dog and gather up the dirt these are impressed upon. Apply this soil to the paralyzed area and rub it in.

Light a fire with a blessed ember and when the coals are good and red throw a dog's flea on them as you continue to rub the dirt on the patient.

To keep a woman from going to A romantic rendez-vous

Burn a lizard in a sandstone pot, and when it is reduced to ashes place the resulting residue in the horn of a billy-goat that was slaughtered on the new moon. On the day when the lady is meant to go to the meeting, trace three lines in front of the door with the ash thus prepared and she will not be able to set foot outside of her house until the sun rises.

To avoid the curse from salt or pepper that is spilled by chance.

It is a bad omen to knock over the salt cellar. To counteract this omen you must take a pinch of the spilt salt between the first three fingers of your right hand and throw it over your left shoulder. For pepper you should use the left hand and throw it over your right shoulder.

To give sight to the blind

Take an ounce of consecrated oil and put it in a porcelain oil dispenser that you will have boiled one hour before to be certain of its cleanliness. Put a ring on the patient's finger that is made from gold and adorned with the birthstone appropriate to his horoscope. Anoint the ring with the oil and hold it between your fingers of Venus and Jupiter (see the book "Chiromancy") Massage the patient's eyelids gently with the oil and remove the ring from his hand, then wipe it with a fine cambric cloth that will be consecrated after this ritual in the manner described elsewhere (see the book "Spells"). Leave a plaster on the eyelids overnight made from the yolks of titmouse eggs and some sparrow dung mixed with the herbs indicated by the planetary correspondences found in my book on *Spells.*

Against intestinal worms

Wrap the hairs from a cow's tail around a bamboo wand from right to left. With this done cut the wand into pieces and burn them. Have the patient come and inhale the smoke. Now have him face the south and sprinkle some sand upon him with your left hand.

Against skin ailments

Massage the afflicted region with cow dung and then some tincture of colocynth or indigo.

Against grey hair

Shave the area where grey hair is growing and apply the preceding formula.

For stomach cramps.

To ease stomach cramps burn some grape vines on the day and at the hour of Mercury. Pronounce the oraison of the Salamanders (see "Spells", part 3) and heat some red wool over it. When the wool catches fire apply it to the stomach and pronounce the oraison appropriate to the day (see our "Complete Grimoires"). Repeat this operation thrice and between applications of the hot wool place a few drops of the balm of the Atharva Veda on the belly, spreading it around with your finger of Jupiter and up to the chest following the flow of the circulation.

Protecting the Harvest from Hail

Procure the horn of a bull and fill it with holy water, then hurl it at the sky powerfully while pronouncing imprecations against storms and hail.

Repeat this practice thrice daily for the next three days upon the rising of the sun, then at noon, and finally at sunset. On the last day take a walk around the field to be protected. Keeping it on your right ride, walk with your arm stretched forth, your hand open and your palm down, the fingers being straightened and spread apart.

Cut some grain from each corner of the field with a consecrated knife. Burn this at night in your fireplace along with some straw from a thatched roof.

Hemorrhages

Touch the area of the heart with a bamboo wand and trace five knots. Give the patient shards of broken glass taken from a demolished house in the form of a talisman. Mix some holy water with some sour milk, throw in four grains of millet and a handful of sesame. Have the patient drink the mixture from the horn of a cow which slipped and fell to its death. This formula is also suitable for women whose menses are too abundant.

Against snakebite

The victim of the bite should wear an amulet made from the skin of a stillborn calf. The satchel should be filled with some dirt from an ant mound. Make a ball with some turf and some ant's eggs which the afflicted man shall then place in his right nostril with his right thumb. Now burn the bite area with a flaming yew branch before throwing it onto the guilty serpent or, if this is impossible, onto the ground in the place where the bite occurred.

Finally place a mix of borage and butter under the arches of the victim's feet and massage the bite area following the flow of circulation from low to high. Feed the victim some honey from the tip of a porcupine's quill and have him drink some holy water from a Calabash.

To triumph over rivals

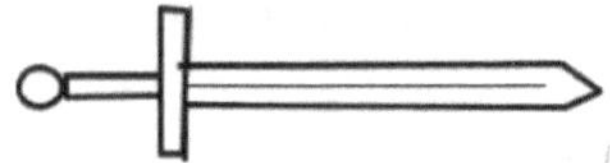

Procure some cord made from hemp gathered on the day of Venus and twisted during the full moon of September. Cut it into as many pieces as there are other men courting your beloved.

Take all of the fragments out at night as the moon is rising and shove them into cracks in the walls of the homes where your rivals reside. Go and retrieve them seven days later at the same time and place them in a bottle that you shall plug with a new cork and cover with some consecrated blue wax. Set the bottle on a raft made of elderberry branches and allow the raft to carry the bottle away downstream.

To tame birds

Cook the left paw of a three-colored cat in a pot with some consecrated honey and some hemp seeds crushed between two rocks from a riverbed.

Cut the paw into fourths and envelope these in grape leaves, knotting them with a piece of white horsehair. Attach the first packet to the foot of a pigeon and let him fly off at noon. Put the second packet in a swallow's nest. Put the third deep in the woods in the fork of a tree formed by three branches. Keep the fourth. Each of these operations shall be done on its own day, and on the morning of the fourth day you shall pronounce the **oraison of the sylphs** while holding the last packet in hand, at which point birds will come from everywhere and land on you as a friend.

A Deadly Curse to be used against A dire enemy

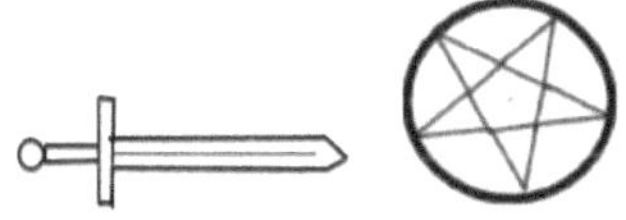

Find your way into his presence and when you get the chance drop a stone into the area covered by his shadow. It is best if he is walking toward the south. When he is gone go and find his left footprint. Take a cypress wand the tip of which you have sharpened with your magic dagger and bisect the footprint longitudinally and crosswise, then draw diagonals until you have made six lines. Take up the dirt that is moved through this process and fold it in a rhubarb leaf. Do this to a second left footprint and you should have enough dirt.

Go home and light a fire on the day and at the hour of *Mars* on a night of the new moon, then throw the dirt on the fire. Your enemy will surely meet with misfortune, and if the dirt should cause sparks when thrown upon the flames it means that he shall be killed by illness or accident soon.

To put a curse on your Enemy's food

Begin preparing for the spell some twelve days before by mixing some barley meal with some hot water. For the first three days throw in three handfuls of barley, on the second three days add two, and on the remaining six days add one handful. Each time you make this preparation you must drink it down at one gulp. On the 13th day have your enemy eat a plate of rice or bowl of rice porridge as early as possible. The plate you serve him with should be one recently used by a starving man, and you will first heap it with the vilest curses and maledictions. It is best if you have remnants of the starving man's meal to mix in with the rice. When your enemy is done eating throw any leftover rice in a pond where there are many fish. If the fish come up immediately to feed your spell is a complete success. A terrible indigestion will seize your enemy and then he will die.

To bring happiness into a new house.

On the day and at the hour of Jupiter during the waning of the moon you must light a fire with some green wood after peeling off the bark and pronouncing the **exorcism of fire** and the **oraison of Salamanders**. When the fire is blazing you must burn two old shoes. You will have all of the happiness you hoped for when you acquired the new house.

To get to sleep

You must whistle toward the four corners of the room in which you sleep and make as if to write the four divine names shown below in the four corners with your index finger:

Adonay, Eloym, Agla, Tetragrammaton. Now lay on your back with your arms over the side of the bed with the palms of your hands turned outward.

A curse to rob a man of sleep

On three consecutive nights you must pass before the victim's door such that you are facing the doorstep when the clock strikes 12:30, 1:00, and 1:30. On the 4th night light a red lantern if there is no moon and sketch on his door with a consecrated pencil the **double triangle of Solomon.** Acquire 12 black pins and a white pin with a red head. With these you will affix 13 dead flies to the door such that there is one at each point of the star of Solomon, one at each intersection of the lines, and one at the center (the red and white pin). The person who is the object of this spell shall not sleep until the end of the lunar month.

END